May, 2

Katie,

The author of this book
is our own Sylvester T. Gillespie.
A 1962 graduate of Rust College.
Pastor of John Wesley United Methodist
Church -- 1968 - 1975.
Enjoy the book —
Annette

The Lighthouse of Words

My Spiritual Journey from Abandonment to Divine Appointment

Sylvester T. Gillespie

iUniverse®

THE LIGHTHOUSE OF WORDS
MY SPIRITUAL JOURNEY FROM ABANDONMENT
TO DIVINE APPOINTMENT

32 Scriptures, King James Version, The Westley Study Bible, and The New International Version

King James Version (KJV)
Public Domain

New International Version (NIV)
Holy Bible, New International Version®, NIV® Copyright ©1973, 1978, 1984, 2011 by Biblica, Inc.® Used by permission. All rights reserved worldwide.

New Revised Standard Version Bible, copyright © 1989 National Council of the Churches of Christ in the United States of America. Used by permission. All rights reserved worldwide.

iUniverse books may be ordered through booksellers or by contacting:

iUniverse
1663 Liberty Drive
Bloomington, IN 47403
www.iuniverse.com
1-800-Authors (1-800-288-4677)

ISBN: 978-1-5320-4652-0 (sc)
ISBN: 978-1-5320-4653-7 (e)

Library of Congress Control Number: 2018904531

Print information available on the last page.

iUniverse rev. date: 04/16/2018

Quotes of Vince Lombardi was printed off the internet from http://www.goodreads.com/author/quotes/9771155/32550Vince_LombardiJr

Quotes of president Barack Obama taken from the internet https://www.brainyquote.com/quotes/authors/b/arack_obama.htm

Quote of first lady Michelle Obama speaks following a screening of the movie, "Hidden Figures," in the Eisenhower Executive Office Building adjacent to the White House on December 15, 2016. Saul Loeb—AFP/Getty Images

Quote on the "Morning Joe television program," President Obama stated "that his most treasured line in the Good Book is taken from Isaiah 40:31."

Quotes of Mr. Gaddafi from the internet/ www.azquotes.com Author/5263-Muammar_al_Gaddafi

Quotes of Mr. Sadat www.netfind.com/SadatQuotes

Words from song "The Impossible Dream" lyrics: Lyrics by Joe Darion In this song, Quixote explains his quest and the reasons behind it. In doing so, he captures the essence as sung by the cast of the Man of La Mancha. https://www.stlyrics.com/lyrics/ … /theimpossibledream.htm

Tyson, Timothy B., Blood Done Sign My Name (New York: Three Rivers Press, 2004), 103-105.

Contents

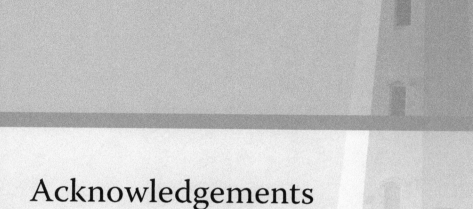

Acknowledgements

I wish to acknowledge all of the people, personalities and contributors who are too numerous to name. Many of them hold a special place within my heart and are named on pages 92 and 93 as they were most helpful in sharing my deepest thoughts and assisting in finalizing these written pages.

Special Thanks

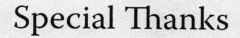

*I*t is with sincere gratitude and special thanks that I acknowledge the progress of this project that has been facilitated through the extraordinary generosity of the following persons. May Almighty God bless and enrich each of your lives, for believing in my dream and supporting me in this effort. They are:

Captain Samuel M. and Mrs. Bettye Dacus
Members of Saint Mark United Methodist Church
Los Angeles, CA.

Mr. Lloyd and the late Mrs. Katherine Watson
Members of Scott United Methodist Church
Pasadena, CA.

Foreword

*W*hen one reads the life reflections of a person, it should be done with reverence, especially if they are from of a person of the Spirit, like the Reverend Sylvester T. Gillespie. Indeed, it is like overhearing a private conversation one is having with God. In fact, he titles this volume *The Lighthouse of Words*. But if a reader pays attention to only Gillespie's words, he or she will miss so much he intends to convey, for the writer often allows others to speak for him. And those words are as important to understanding his soul as the eloquent and revealing ones he chooses. So it is crucial when reading these life reflections not to skip over something that might appear at a quick glance to be filler or not especially relevant. And don't read too fast! One should take great care when looking into the soul of another, especially when it is borne with such candor and utter honesty.

Early on, you will find that these reflections seek transparency. The author begins his story with these words: "I was born on May 23, 1938, to a young fourteen-year-old girl named Fanny Kate

Jones." Here it is: Stark. Jarring. Naked truth. Words from the soul. This is Rev. Sylvester T. Gillespie's story. Not mine. Not yours. The value to be gained in its reading is to allow it to be uniquely his. That is what happened to me. I walked with him, laughed with him, and cried with him. I sought to know his mind—but more his soul, as he intended. Looking into another soul is serious business.

What the good reverend has cleverly done is to suggest that if we are to understand him better, we must sometimes look not at him but elsewhere: what music he likes, what sports teams he roots for, what angers him, what scriptures touch his soul, and what songs move him. It was Tennyson, I believe, who said, "I am a part of all that I have known." So these soul renderings are whole. They come from not only the sanctuary but the streets and sounds of life. Most importantly, they come from an African American United Methodist preacher who desires that the world know the depth of his faith and love for God and *all* God's people. Rev. Sylvester T. Gillespie's spiritual reflections have found a resting place in my spirit. May it be so for all who read this volume.

Bishop Woodie W. White, Retired
The United Methodist Church
Atlanta, Georgia
September 17, 2017

A Salute to My Spiritual Heroes

Spiritual Collaborator
Bishop Woodie W. White

The name Woodie has the power of attraction, allurement, and magnetism across the United Methodist Church (the second-largest protestant denomination in America). To refer to Bishop White as *Bishop White*, a number of people in the denomination may not know who you are referring to, but when you say *Woodie*, there is no question as to whom you are talking about. The name Woodie does not indicate a lack of respect, but rather, for many African Americans in the church, it is to signify a sense of comradeship, friendship, and fellowship with a bishop within the United Methodist Church.

Bishop White was appointed as the first general secretary of the United Methodist Commission on Religion and Race. From 1968 until 1984, he had two associates—the late Dr. Clayton Hammond and Dr. Albert Hammond (not related)—who traveled the highways and byways, healing the division of racism across United Methodism. Bishop White was elected as bishop by the North Central Jurisdiction in 1984 and assigned to the Illinois area. After eight years as presiding bishop of the Illinois area, he was assigned to be a presiding bishop of the Indiana area in 1992. Bishop White retired as an active bishop in the United Methodist Church in 2004, and following his retirement, he became a professor at the world-renowned Emory University located in Atlanta, Georgia.

Spiritual Counselor
Rev. Dr. Zan W. Holmes Jr.

Dr. Zan Holmes is known across United Methodism as one of the most gifted clergy persons, and he is one of America's greatest preachers and pastors. Over a period of forty-three years in the ministry, Dr. Holmes is known to have grown the membership from fifty members to more than six thousand during his twenty-eight years as pastor at St. Luke Community United Methodist Church in Dallas, Texas.

Dr. Holmes has served as a Texas state representative, as a district superintendent, a presenter of the United Methodist Disciple Bible Study Course, and as a professor of preaching at Perkins Divinity School of Theology at the world-renowned Southern Methodist University (SMU) located in Dallas, Texas.

Spiritual Confidant
Rev. Dr. Cecil L. Murray

No clergy person in the city of Los Angeles is more revered, respected, or honored than the Rev. Dr. Cecil L. "Chip" Murray. He is affectionately referred to as Chip across the Christian, religious, and educational communities within Los Angeles where he is like a magnet that draws the best out of people.

Dr. Murray was appointed to First African Methodist Episcopal Church (FAME) of Los Angeles in 1977. At that time, the membership was approximately three hundred parishioners, which increased to more than eighteen thousand during his tenure and prior to his retirement in 2004. Since then, he has been serving as a professor in the Center for Religion at the world-renowned University of Southern California (USC) in Los Angeles, California, and he is a best-selling author of *Twice Tested by Fire: A Memoir of Faith and Service* published in 2012.

Introduction

Words to me can be likened to a candle that frightens away the darkness. When I'm all alone and feeling kind of blue and there is no one except God to shout out my troubles to, words are always there to comfort, inspire, encourage, and revive my innerness and my soul. I thank God always for poets, scholars, and authors who have taken simple words and painted such magnificent pictures. I have never heard words say, "I cannot light any more of your darkness." Never heard a word say such a thing. When I personally have gotten lost under God's painted gray skies, the words of poets have helped me understand that *tomorrow will come and who knows what the tide will bring.* I hardly remember in detail word-for-word any poet, writer, or speaker I have read or heard, but it is the ideas that came from their work that have taken up residence in the canyons of my mind, and I've tried to draw words from them.

I hope you enjoy *My Lighthouse of Words.*

Where My
Abandonment Began

I was born on May 23, 1938, to a young fourteen-year-old girl named Fanny Kate Jones. Because there was no father's name on my birth certificate, I was given the name of Sylvester Poe and did not know that my last name was Gillespie until several years later, when my birth certificate was located in the county courthouse in Starkville, Mississippi. I was told that my birth mother was identified as a young, pregnant wanderer who had no place to stay. Robert and Becky Poe, an elderly couple in the community of Plair, were known to give a helping hand to many destitute and displaced young persons. My birth mother was no exception, and they offered her a place to stay in their shabby country home during her pregnancy.

Upon my birth, assisted by a midwife, Mr. and Mrs. Poe told my mother, "Girl, you may stay here as long as you wish, but if or when you choose to leave, you cannot take this baby with you, because you are only a baby yourself."

After she was strong enough, she made the decision to leave me in the safe environment with Robert and Becky Poe … and she was never to be heard from or seen again during my seventy-nine years of life.

Several years later (maybe when I was eight or nine years old), the midwife who had delivered me saw me and said, "You know what, boy? Your mama never did pay me for delivering you."

What a terrible thing to say to a young boy. But she never forgot that debt, and I never forgot her reminding me of the unpaid debt.

After the deaths of Mama and Daddy Poe, I became what was called the community's lost boy because I, like my mother, became a wanderer. And because no one stepped forward to guide, love, or care for me, I felt all alone in this world as I wandered around in the community of Plair totally lost. I was the picking post in the community, and it seemed that all the youngsters picked on me. I was their teasing post, their laughing post, their ridiculing post, and their abusing post. I don't believe they were trying to cause me pain. This was just something amusing for them to do, but it certainly was not amusing to me. The only boy who stuck up for me was named James Wallace Knox, and a number of times we were both beaten up as he defended me.

My friend James Wallace played a pivotal part in my decision to go into the ministry. I thought that he was going to become a preacher because his father, Rev. Jessie James Knox, was a local preacher at Plair Methodist Church, and I did not want him to become a preacher before I did. So I made it known within the community that I wanted to preach because I didn't want to be known as a copycat.

The elderly people in the Plair community began saying, "He's gonna be a preacher." It made me happy and excited to be called the little preacher because this title gave me a little more self-esteem, and it kept me from being beaten up all the time.

There was a white lady named Mrs. Molly Rutherford who owned the only country store in the community of Plair. She heard that I wanted to become a preacher, so she bought me my first Bible. When she gave it to me, she instructed me to never tell her husband, Mr. Andrew Rutherford, about this gift, and I never did. The gift was very special to me, and I appreciated the Bible given to me by Mrs. Rutherford.

Then it happened during the summer of 1950. I was around twelve years of age when both the late Reverend W. B. Rogers, pastor of Plair Methodist Church, and presiding elder Reverend B. F. Harper apparently called the late Bishop Robert E. Jones and his wife, Mrs. Elizabeth Jones, to allow me to enroll in the Gulfside Assembly Boys School, which was located in Waveland, Mississippi. Bishop Jones was founder of Gulfside Assembly and the first African American elected bishop in the Methodist Church.

Bishop and Mrs. Jones had organized a school for poor, rural, underprivileged boys, known as the Gulfside Poor Boys' School, where I was later allowed to attend. This was the first time I really felt like I was a part of a family, and more importantly, I knew where my next meal was coming from.

This period of time was during the dark days in the Deep South when segregation was prominent and Gulfside was the only place where African Americans could come and hold their large meetings, interface, and network with one another. The summer months were the peak times for organizations to hold their meetings from across the Central Jurisdiction (a jurisdiction for all African Americans) in the Methodist Church across the Deep South.

The Gulfside boys, along with some college students, made up the summer workforce at the Gulfside Poor Boys' School. Some of the students worked in the dining hall, some were assigned to work on beautifying the lawn, and others were assigned to keep the buildings clean. There were several stately white buildings that had been built on the Gulfside campus that always needed to appear neat and clean. Those buildings were named after great African

American Methodist leaders, such as Brooks Chapel, Jones Hall, Longmore Inn, Graff Hall, and Hooser Hall, along with several other beautiful buildings throughout the campus.

During the summers, I became known as Sylvester, the Go-To Boy. It simply meant that if people needed their floors mopped, their bed linens changed, their trash cans emptied, their clothes taken to the laundry, or their commodes unstopped, all they needed to do was find Sylvester. I would get the job done for them.

Among the many leaders who came to Gulfside to lecture or teach during the summer months were scholars and preachers, such as Earnest Smith, Robert Hayes, W. T. Handy, John Graham, James Peters, W. S. P. Norris, Robert Harrington, William R. London, Joe Washington, Alfred Norris, Garfield Owens, Zan Holmes, B.F. Harper, D.T. Jackson, James C. Peters, Mason Peters and many others. I simply adored all those great scholars and pastors.

I suppose that I must have stood out to one couple, Charles and Ida Golden, because they believed in me. Perhaps it was because of my work ethic. They adopted me as their foster son, and the rest is history. These two people cared for and loved me as if I were their biological son. If there is such a thing as going from rags to riches, I am a prime example. I know that the Lord was in this plan because He was in total control of my life, wants, and needs.

Years after my adoption, I enrolled in Rust College in Holly Springs, Mississippi, during the fall of 1958, and I graduated in 1962. If any of my classmates from those years are still alive, they would vouch for my dress code. During my four years at Rust College, I was voted president of my freshman class and also president of my junior class. I was far from being known as any kind of great scholar, but I certainly was known as a good dresser, and it was all because of Charles and Ida Golden. Oh, by the way, I received my bachelor of arts from Rust College and my master of divinity from Gammon Theology Seminary of the Interdenominational Theological Center located in Atlanta, Georgia.

Now, I know that some reading this story might question my call to the ministry and may even wonder whether I am sure God called me. Others may even be thinking that perhaps it was James Wallace Knox who called me to preach. But please understand that I thoroughly believe in the old saying that God almighty works in mysterious ways, His wonders to perform. Although the late James Wallace Knox never became a minister, he certainly inspired me. I have actively been preaching the Gospel for more than forty years. In 2018, I will be eighty years of age, and guess what? I can still cut a preaching rug every now and then.

While doing a self-evaluation, I recognize that I am not as good as I once was, but I am as good once as I ever was. And now I can say to my friend James Wallace Knox, who I believe is in heaven, "Old friend, I'll catch up with you later down the road."

My Family

Dedication
To my loving wife,
the late Barbara Bonney Gillespie

My Barbara

My Barbara

*T*here were various life-changing challenges that occurred during my pastoral appointment at Wesley United Methodist Church in Los Angeles, California. Through the grace of almighty God, He sent me one of His special angels to walk with me and prop me up after a devastating divorce. I credit my Barbara for helping God to save my ministry. I looked fairly decent on the outside, but I was really messed up spiritually on the inside until God sent her to rescue me. When she finished polishing me up spiritually, it was time for her to go home to be with the Lord.

It was through the caring inspiration and everlasting loving memory of my late wife, friend, and confidante, my Barbara (the name I so fondly called her), whom will remain forever in my heart. Her ongoing love and encouragement were always expressed in a quiet and reassuring manner. She remains vibrantly in my heart and soul as I share this, my extended dedication in her loving memory. She was my silent partner who often experienced my many heavy burdens, as she always encouraged and supported my every move with inspiration as a pastor doing God's work. She was my sounding board when I needed her to be and my shield who kept me grounded, and with her melodious voice and kindness, we helped so many in the church.

A Tribute to My Sons

While the road was tough during my first marriage, every time I thought about giving up my ministry, my two beautiful Gillespie sons (now men, Dekovan T., fifty-one years of age, and Damian T., forty-nine years of age) became my guardian angels of sorts, inasmuch as their presence always reminded me that my calling required strength in the midst of this storm. It was important that I, as their father, provide them a pleasant family environment. Thus, we spent many happy times together, just my two boys and me.

Our favorite source of fun included many Friday nights at the drive-in theater where we enjoyed many scary movies, which all three of us liked to watch. We always looked forward to going to the drive-in theater on Friday nights. We had so much fun making preparation to see the scary movies in our car. We covered up with quilts, ate our home-cooked bologna sandwiches, and sipped our homemade Kool-Aid drinks. We were low on cash, so I had to improvise, adapt, and overcome not having enough money to purchase hot dogs and popcorn from the drive-in concession stand. But my young sons seem to understand our financial situation, and they never questioned why I was unable to buy goodies. We all just enjoyed being together as we watched the scary movies. We had lots of great times during our special Friday-night fun times.

In fact, it was so obvious to many of the members at John Wesley UMC in Fayetteville, North Carolina, that they started calling my two boys and me the three musketeers simply because of our close relationship. That bond continues today even though they have families of their own. Up until just a few years ago, their wives would allow the three of us to meet at my home in Los Angeles, where we would make plans to resume our special bonding time. We planned some great touring sites in Monterey and various surrounding Northern California areas near Fort Ord, where I spent two years of active military duty. We usually stopped in Santa Barbara, Santa Rosa, San Louis Obispo, Fort Hunter Liggett, and a number of other smaller areas where we would stop to eat, tour, and even see scary movies, just as we did when they were little boys.

Yes, I thank God for Dekovan and Damian—my two sons who were previously referred to as the other two musketeers. They were, in reality, my much-needed inspirational anchor during my restless, unsettled, and uneasy spirit when I was so much in need of peace within.

I love you, my two boys!
Dad

Prayers from the Author's Heart

A flower waits for the falling rain and experiences the dryness of a drought. But the flower keeps its face turned toward heaven and is refreshed the next morning because it made itself available for the presence of the dew. So do we, oh God, lift up the faces of our hearts toward heaven for the falling rain of Your blessings. Bless us and keep us. Amen.

A cup of sunshine, a thimble of snow, a daffodil, a leaf turning gold—this much of God I know. The God who flung the heavens into space and hung the stars upon the canopy of blue. The God who let the dewdrops of heaven kiss the roses and pinned the curtain of night behind the stars. The God who, without a ladder, without a brush, painted the heaven blue and said, "This will be My throne." The God who made the sun and the stars and then took the scraps from making the sun and made the moon. When we feel, oh God, that we have been ripped off, roughed up, and run down by the weights, the cares, and the worries of the world and we are left depleted, diminished, battled, and broken, we remember the words of Albert Schweitzer: "He comes to us as One unknown, without a name, as of old, by the lakeside ... He will reveal Himself in the toils, the conflicts, the sufferings which they shall pass through in His fellowship." Amen.

Breathe on my words, oh God, make my words Your words, and rescue me from me. Love me and do anything You wish to do with me. You can be reckless with me without my permission. Hide me behind the cross so that people might see You and not me. Amen.

Who am I, Lord? Am I what men tell of, or am I what I know of myself to be? Am I living my life as a tale told by an idiot full of sound and fury, signifying nothing? Who am I, Lord? Am I evasive, irritable, rude, offensive, insulting, or repugnant? Who am I, Lord? Am I a trap, a fake, a cheat, a liar, a fraud, or a counterfeit? Who am I, Lord? Now, Lord, I know that I have asked this question so many times regarding my true identity, but now I realize that whosoever I am, Lord, I am Thine. So hold me, mold me, make me, heal me, and help me to take on all the attributes of You so that I may walk like You, talk like You, act like You, and be like You. Amen.

Is Prayer your steering wheel or is Prayer your spare tire? Amen

Words, Personal Quotes
and Scriptures to Live By

If every man would give a thread, every poor man would have a shirt.

Never deal in small talk, because small talk develops into little lies.

The me I see is the me I'll be. If I cannot see it, I will never be it ... Until I believe it, I will never achieve it.

The direction you are going is more important than the distance you have come from.

Fear knocked, faith answered the door, but no one was there.

The soul would never have a rainbow if the eyes never had a tear.

You can believe anything in this world; just don't claim to be right.

Belief versus Believe: Mark 9:23 KJV
Jesus said unto him, If thou canst believe, all things are possible to him that believeth.

Belonging

This earth is my temporary home; it's not where I belong. It**'s only windows and rooms; it's just a stop on my way to where I'm going. I am not afraid, because I know this is my temporary home.**

Belong versus Belonging: Romans 8:9 KJV
But ye, however, are not in the flesh but in the Spirit, if in fact the Spirit of God dwells in you. Now if anyone does not have the Spirit of Christ he is not His.

Church

I believe my church—the United Methodist Church—is coming apart at the seam ... The seam is God; when you unstitch the seam, the garment is going to fall apart.

The church for many people is a part of their social lives; it is a place to be involved and to do something. After all, you can meet some good people down at the church.

The church must never be a snooty, religious country club that starts at eleven o'clock sharp and ends at noon. Dull.

The church must be more than a place where the congregation gets no more than a relational, religious pep talk.

Many of our churches are refrigerators of religion instead of incubators of life.

Members of the church are called to be spiritual midwives, helping people to be born again!

When the church is overorganized, it suffocates the spirit.

If every United Methodist would dust off his or her Bible at the same time, we would have the worst dust storm in history.

If I had not been saved by the grace of God, but instead I was a burdened, down-and-out stranger when visiting some of our United Methodist Churches since my retirement as a pastor, I would have walked out of the worship service saying, "I won't be back." Because I'm already down enough, and I just don't need to be down anymore.

In some of our churches, the spirit of the congregation resembles the faces chiseled out on Mount Rushmore with Boris Karloff at the organ.

For God's sake ... Where is the power among us that releases, liberates, forgives, frees, heals, and saves? For God's sake, where is the power?!

Church: Colossians 1:24 KJV

Who now rejoice in my sufferings for you, and fill up that which is behind of the afflictions of Christ in my flesh for his body's sake, which is the church.

There is a squirrel in every family tree—jumpy, jittery, and agitating.

Never let the buzzards of discord build their nasty nest in your home or your life.

If we are ever to love a butterfly, we must care for a few caterpillars.

You don't need a hatchet to kill a gnat on the forehead of another person.

You don't need a sledgehammer to crack a nut.

Some people will use you but really don't have any use for you … except for what they can get out of you, and then they will discard you.

Some people are parasites living on the emotions of good people.

Clever Expressions: Creatures of the Earth: Genesis 1:24 KJV
And God said, Let the earth bring forth the living creatures after his kind, cattle, and creeping thing, and beast of the earth after his kind: and it was so.

Cutting Words

Cutting words through careless lips, softly spoken ... Oh, you can do damage and never scream or shout. Emotions get the best of us, and we say things we don't mean ... And it's too late to take 'em back once they are out.

It only takes a breath or two to tear your world apart. Sticks and stones may break your bones, but words can break your heart.

—Don Henley

Cutting Words: Matthew 12:36 KJV
But I say unto you, That every idle word that men shall speak, they shall give account thereof in the day of judgment.

Change what you can, and manage what you can't.

There is no gain without pain. Think not of what you have lost but what you have left, and your scars will be turned into stars.

Christians live by what they believe and not by what they feel.

If you are satisfied with your life the way it is, you are in trouble because to be content is to have no dream. When you have no dream, you die. Woe unto those who are at ease in Zion.

Never allow too many people to have too much access to your personal life.

Discernment: 1 Kings 3:9 KJV
Spiritual direction and understanding—the ability to judge well.
Give therefore thy servant an understanding heart to judge thy people, that I may discern between good and bad: for who is able to judge this thy so great a people?

Faith

Faith and fear do not go together; they cannot be in the same room, to say nothing about being roommates.

Faith does not require a backup plan.

I can tell a whole lot about your faith by the way you're willing to talk about death.

Faith: 2 Corinthians 5:7 KJV
For we walk by faith, not by sight.

God

God is my pilot light. He is my medicine cabinet, and He is my nightingale.

Do not magnify your problem; magnify God … because He is bigger than your problem.

God does not have anything in His inventory that is small enough for a lazy person to do.

God does not judge us for what we do not know, but He judges us for what we do know and reject.

I'm at peace because I have made the decision in this upside-down world that God is the same yesterday, today, and forever.

God is always your brand-new second chance.

Man elevates, but God deflates.

God: John 3:16 KJV
For God so loved the world, that he gave his only begotten Son, that whosoever believeth in him should not perish, but have everlasting life.

Quarreling over which denomination is closer to God is like two ants fighting over which ant is going to eat the dead elephant.

If everybody is coming back from wherever you are going, either you are on a one-way street, or whatever meeting you were going to is over.

Grace: 1 Corinthians 15:10 KJV
A special virtue, gift, or help given by God.
But by the grace of God I am what I am: and his grace which was bestowed upon me was not in vain; but I labored more abundantly than they all: yet not I, but the grace of God that is with me.

Job asked God many questions, to which he got no answers. But in his questions, he got more of God.

If I had not been saved by the "Grace of God" and instead I was a burdened down and out stranger and found myself in some of our United Methodist Churches that I have attended since my retirement as a pastor . . . as I walked out of the worship service, I have said to myself, "I won't be back because I am down enough and I just don't need to be down anymore."

If you have been saved by the Grace of God, you don't need to call a committee to make a decision. You need to *just do it.*

Grace of God: 1 Peter 4:10 KJV
As every man hath received the gift, even so minister the same one to another, as good stewards of the manifold grace of God.

Holy Spirit

If I could bottle up and sell the Holy Spirit, I could clean up and heal every drug dealer and user on the streets of this world.

If you have the Holy Spirit and do not feel the Holy Spirit, you can lose the Holy Spirit and never knew you had the Holy Spirit.

He that hath no rule over his own spirit is like a city that is broken without walls.

The Holy Spirit must guide and direct your life, and you must be obedient to the Lord.

Holy Spirit: Romans 15:13 KJV
Now the God of hope fill you with all joy and peace in believing, that ye may abound in hope, through the power of the Holy Ghost.

Important Words

The most important words in the English language are *how are you*, *thank you*, and *I love you*.

A lighthouse does not make any noise, but we see it.

Soon it will be illegal and a crime for you to stand alone.

We are forever troubled, pestered, annoyed, and tormented by the tempestuous winds of life. Many of us live at the corner of worry and work. What's your address?

If you don't have anything to do, don't do it here.
—Bishop Charles E. Blake

There ain't no distance for a stepper.
—Tex Felder

Important Words: 1 Corinthians 2:13 KJV
Utterance, communications, statements, or expressions.
Which things also we speak, not in the words which man's wisdom teacheth, but which the Holy Ghost teacheth; comparing spiritual things with spiritual.

Inner Peace

There were times in my life when I felt my life was like a car speeding down the highway in the fast lane, and I was in the back seat.

A friend multiplies your joy and divides your pain.

Don't nest on the crest. Find fountains on the mountains.

Let no one tell you how high you can fly. Go ahead. Climb the mountain and look the eagle in the eye.

Is prayer your steering wheel, or is prayer your spare tire?

Inner Peace: Romans 14:19 KJV
Let us therefore follow after the things which make for peace, and things wherewith one may edify another.

If Jesus is bold, brazen, and bodacious enough to declare that "I am the Way, the Truth, and the Life," either He is a liar, He is a lunatic, or He is Lord.

I was not there when Jesus walked on the water. I was not there when Jesus calmed the raging sea. I was not there when He healed and cleansed the lepers. I was not there, and I did not see, but I believe.

I know Jesus cares for us because He said in His word He would supply all our needs according to His riches in glory. I know He is rich because He said in His word He owns the cattle of a thousand hills. He also said in His word, "the earth is the Lord's and the fullness thereof." He said in his word, "The Lord is my light and my salvation; whom shall I fear? The Lord is the strength of my life; of whom shall I be afraid?" (Ps. 27:1 KJV). So all we have to do is kick back, relax, and rest in His word.

The world offers promises full of emptiness. The tomb offers emptiness full of promises because of Jesus's resurrection.

Jesus paid for our sins through the crucifixion, and He got the receipt through the resurrection.

I am trying to live my life as if Jesus died yesterday, rose today, and is coming back tomorrow.

Talking about Jesus without having a personal relationship with Him is simply spiritual static.

Jesus Christ is the same yesterday, and today, and forever.

Jesus: Philippians 4:19 KJV
But my God will supply all your need according to his riches in glory by Christ Jesus.

Knowledge

I would rather be biblically correct than politically correct.

I would rather fail trying than be the biggest and the most successful nothing in the world.

A wish changes nothing. A decision changes everything.

It's difficult to receive the truth when you hear what you want to hear.

Never allow the rules to overrule your common sense.

Knowledge: 2 Peter 1:2 KJV
Grace and peace be multiplied unto you through the knowledge of God, and of Jesus our Lord.

Leader

Barack Hussein Obama
Forty-fourth president of the United States of America
January 20, 2009–January 20, 2017

The forty-fourth commander in chief of the United States, President Barack Hussein Obama, is quoted as saying, "If you're walking down the right path and you're willing to keep walking, eventually you'll make progress."

While president of the United States, on Friday, June 30, 2017, during the *Morning Joe* television program, President Obama stated that his most treasured line in the Good Book is taken from Isaiah 40:31.

"But they that wait upon the Lord shall renew their strength; they shall mount up with wings as eagles; they shall run, and not be weary; and they shall walk, and not faint."

Michelle Robinson Obama
Former first lady of the United States of America

In her last speech as first lady, she said the following: "I want our young people to know that they matter; that they belong. So don't be afraid. Do you hear me? Young people don't be afraid. Be focused. Be determined. Be hopeful. Be empowered. Empower yourselves with a good education. Then get out there and use that education to build a country worthy of your boundless promise. Lead by example with hope, never fear, and know that I will be with you, rooting for you and working to support you for the rest of my life."

As seen through my eyes, her grace, charm, and beauty are astonishing, startling, and astounding. She has the eloquence of a swan. —Sylvester T. Gillespie

But in the evening of my memory, always I come back to West Point. Always I hear the echoes and re-echoes: Duty, Honor, and Country. Today marks my final roll call with you, but I want you to know that when I cross the river my last conscious thoughts will be of The Corps, and The Corps, and The Corps. I bid you farewell.
—Gen. Douglas MacArthur

I would rather have a player on my team that makes the team greater, than a great player.
—Coach John Wooden

> Christians are wounded soldiers limping their way home.
> You can't be a leader if you don't have any followers.
> You don't need a leader if you don't plan to go anywhere.

Leadership: Proverbs 11:14 KJV
Where no counsel is, the people fall: but in the multitude of counselors there is safety.

Life

Life is not the breath you take, but life is the moments that take your breath away.

Life is a dance you learn as you go. Sometimes you lead; sometimes you follow. Don't worry about what you don't know, because life is a dance you learn as you go.

Life is a mystery to be lived, not a problem to be solved.

Life is what happens to you as you make other plans.

Life: Romans 8:6 KJV
For to be carnally minded is death; but to be spiritually minded is life and peace.

Longevity

At the age of seventy-nine, I'm rocking in my rocking chair, pointed toward the west, but I'm traveling at an easy pace.

Age is not a time of life; it is a state of mind. You are as old as your despair, as young as your dreams.

I am as old as everything I've ever done, and I am as young as everything I want to do.

Growing old is inevitable. Aging is optional.

I started walking the other day. I stopped, and I forgot to start again.

I started walking the other day. I bent down to tie my shoes, and I stayed there wondering what else I could find while I was still bending down.

Longevity: Proverbs 3:16 KJV
Length of days is in her right hand; in her left hand are riches and honor.

Love

Love is kind. Love is blind. Love is yours. Love is mine. Love is not just something that we have, but love is something that we do.

Love ever gives, forgives, outlives, and stands with open hands. And while love lives, it gives, for this is love's prerogative … It gives and gives and gives.

Physical chemistry generates desire. Emotional chemistry generates affection. Mental chemistry generates interest, and spiritual chemistry generates love. It takes all four to create a soul mate.

I am the little pencil in the hand of God, but He does the writing. (by the author but inspired by Mother Teresa of Calcutta)

Love: 1 Corinthians 13:13 KJV
And now abideth faith, hope, charity, these three; but the greatest of these is charity.

– Meaningful Statements about the Devil –

The devil is a lion, and we are his lamb chops.

The devil is not very attractive, and neither is anyone with his last name ... whatever his last name is.

I have proof that the devil exists ... First of all, he exists because the Bible says he does. Secondly, I know he exists because I have had to do some business with 'em.

God does not whip the devil's children. He only whips His own. How do I know that? Proverbs 3:12 says, The Lord disciplines those He loves. But God never wastes a hurt because all things work together for good to them that love God, to them who are the called according to His purpose. (Rom. 8:28)

Mr. Anwar Sadat, the late president of Egypt, said of the late president of Libya, Mr. Muammar Gaddafi, that he was 100 percent crazy or possessed by the devil.

About the Devil: Matthew 25:41 KJV
Then shall he say also unto them on the left hand, Depart from me, ye cursed, into everlasting fire, prepared for the devil and his angels.

Miracle

The greatest miracle is not the one that tricked you (like Harry Houdini), but the greatest miracle is the one that makes you believe in the resurrection of Jesus Christ.

Miracle: Psalm 136:3 KJV
Only He can do great miracles.
O give thanks to the Lord of lords: for his mercy endureth forever.

Pastors

Far too many of us pastors are small in character but big on opinion.
 Far too many of us pastors are overexposed and underachieving.
 Far too many of us pastors are all showcase and no warehouse.
You can win the argument (pastors) but lose the people.

I would rather have a pastor who stumbles, falls, and fails in his or her ministry, but gets up and tries again, than to have a pastor who lives on his or her laurels.
—Bishop Charlie F. Golden

Big doors open up on small hinges. In California, you have to travel through Needles, Blythe, Barstow, and the Mojave Desert before you get to Hollywood. (A lesson for young preachers.)

Shepherds must never allow the church to become keepers of the aquarium, but instead, the church should be fishers of men.

Pastors: Wesleyan Core Team, The Wesley Study Bible, Page 1435 NRSV

John Wesley called Methodist preachers and class leaders "spiritual guides," not pastors. Genuine pastors faithfully care for their flocks so they may grow in both inward and outward holiness.

Perseverance

You cannot change the past, but you can let it go!

Who we are is what we live, what we live is what we sow, and what we sow is what we reap.

I know that I am not to judge you, but I can be a fruit inspector.

This mobile world has killed our personal lives; we have become walkie-talkie zombies.

Perseverance: Ephesians 6:18 KJV
Praying always with all prayer and supplication in the Spirit, and watching thereunto with all perseverance and supplication for all saints.

Rose

If you squeeze a rose, you should not be surprised at the lifelessness of its petals or the odor as it rots.

A thorn defends a rose; it only harms those who would steal the blossom.

We plant seeds in gardens where we may never see the fruit of those seeds.

Rose: Isaiah 35:1 KJV
The wilderness and the solitary place shall be glad for them; and the desert shall rejoice, and blossom as the rose.

Self-Confidence

Never try to outsmart your common sense.

Learn to fly, or your life will be just a free fall.

Keep your face toward the sun, and never look back toward the shadow.

There are two kinds of people in the world: those who build the world and those who just come along and live in it.

Don't expect too much of yourself too soon. Give yourself a chance to grow. Remember: You can't grow yourself. Well, you can grow yourself, but if you do, you will grow yourself crooked. Only God can grow you straight; therefore, don't get too far out in front of yourself.

Self-Confidence: 1 John 3:21 KJV
Beloved, if our heart condemn us not, then have we confidence toward God.

You

You can only do whatever you do only as good as you are.

You can never do things better than you're capable of doing them.

You are only a loser if you quit while you are ahead.

You make a living by what you get; you make a life by what you give.

You have a hard time being anything other than who you are.

What I could do for you is no more than what I should do for you.

You can only protect what you care for, and you can only care for what you understand.

The help you receive to get where you are trying to go is the help you should give back when you get there.

You can never have a perfect day unless you help someone who will never be able to pay you back.

You can always hide behind the certified resume of Jesus Christ.

What you give away you keep, and what you keep you lose.

You may be right, but have you earned the right to say what you think you're right about?

To the world you may be just one person, but to one person you may be the world.

You've got to see before you can be.

Before you can solve a problem, first of all you have to know what the problem is.

You can't impart what you do not possess.

You pray as if you are sending a letter to an unknown address.

You can control your behavior, but you cannot control the outcome of your behavior.

You can't pray your way out of a behavior that you are constantly behaving your way into.

What if you only had today what you only prayed for yesterday?

You: Romans 16:20 KJV
The grace of our Lord Jesus Christ be with you. Amen.

Wisdom

There is no right way to do the wrong thing.

Things work out the best for people who make the best of the way things worked out.

I fail, but my faith does not fail, and when I doubt, faith gets out the eraser.

I always want to be as ignorant as a fool about everything worth learning.

Wisdom: Job 12: 13 KJV
With him is wisdom and strength, he hath counsel and understanding.

A Few Stories as Told
by the Author

Looking Back

*A*s I look back over my life, I realize that I have never been the best at doing anything for the Lord. Now I know perhaps the reader of this story is going to say "Do you mean to tell me that you have been in the ministry for more than forty years, and you have never been the best at doing anything for the Lord? What a sad and tragic note."

I would agree that it's rather pitiful and pathetic for someone to be in the ministry for forty years and say he's never been the best at doing anything for the Lord. Someone might say maybe that person needs to reevaluate his call to Christian ministry.

Let me say to you this: I may never have been the best at doing anything for the Lord during these past forty years in my active ministry, but whatever I have done for the Lord, I tried to do it *well.* You see, you must be very careful when you use the word *best* because the word *best* can inflate you, puff you up, and cause you to become egotistical, narcissistic, or become a me, myself, and I. So if you are going to use the word *best,* make sure it is predicated on Jesus Christ, and then you will know that it is *what you learn*—after you know it all—that counts!

Now these are not my words. These are the words of the late and great John Wooden, who was the magnificent coach of the UCLA Bruins basketball team. John Wooden coached many world-class players, such as Kareem Abdul-Jabbar, Jamaal Wilkes, Keith Erickson, Walt Hazzard, and many other outstanding players. But there was one boy he coached by the name of Bill Walton. Bill was an awesome player, but he had a little problem: he talked quite a bit. Even when he was playing, he was always saying something to the opposing players during the game. But he never downgraded, demeaned, or diminished the other players, because Coach Wooden never would have stood for that.

When Bill graduated from UCLA, Coach Wooden said to him,

"Son, remember when you get your degree and go out into the world, it is what you learn after you know it all that counts." Bill signed a lucrative contract with the Portland Trailblazers of the National Basketball Association (NBA), and he helped the Trailblazers win their only NBA championship. Later, he was traded to the mighty Boston Celtics where he helped the Celtics win another NBA championship to go along with the eleven championships Boston had already won with the help of the Ole Gray Stallion, Mr. Bill Russell.

When Bill Walton retired from the NBA as an active player, he signed on as a basketball analyst for the NBA. Bill Walton was known all over the basketball world as one of the greatest basketball announcers and analysts the league had ever known. One night while he was announcing a game, he began to feel a little sick. After some time had passed, he decided to visit his doctor, but the doctor was unable to determine the nature of his current illness. After Bill continued feeling ill and depressed, he decided to call his old coach. John Wooden was now ninety-nine years of age; he was old, feeble, fragile, frail, and decrepit. But that's all right because who you are is not what you look like on the outside. Who you are is what lives on the inside of what you look like on the outside.

So Coach Wooden listened to Bill's problems, and he said, "Remember, Bill—things work out the best for people who make the best of the way things worked out."

That's biblical because "all things work together for good to them that love God, to them who are the called according to His purpose" (Rom. 8:28; KJV). That's biblical because "weeping may be endure for a night, but joy cometh in the morning" (Ps. 30:5; KJV). And this too is biblical because God plus one makes the majority.

Coach Wooden was a Christian man, not a religious man. There is a great difference between a Christian man and a religious man. A Christian man is a man who has character, and character is who you are when no one else is looking. But a religious man is not concerned about his character. He is only concerned about what other people think about him.

As I have previously said, John Wooden was a Christian man. John courted and dated only one girl during his entire young adult life, and he married her. Her name was Nell, and she and John remained in a loving marriage for fifty-plus years. Interestingly enough, John lived twenty-five years longer after Nell's death, but as John continued to grieve the loss of his wife, he honored her memory by writing a love note to her each month on the date of her death. And after he finished writing his monthly note, he would place those notes in various cracks, crevices, and other special places throughout their condo in Encino, California. Can you imagine how overwhelmed and surprised his daughter must have been when she discovered all the love notes her dad had written to her mother before he passed away? Oh, what an expression of true, devoted love for her mother and his lifelong soul mate.

Man of La Mancha

I saw the play *The Man of La Mancha*. No one knows what Cervantes was trying to say. He wrote in parabolic and allegorical terms because this was the time of the Inquisition, and speaking directly could result in imprisonment or death. But I have my own little thoughts that Miguel de Cervantes had an evangelical encounter with Jesus Christ. Don Quixote was Jesus Christ, Sancho Panza was Peter, My Lady was Mary Magdalene, and the golden helmet was the chalice. The now-famous lyrics read as follows:

> To dream the impossible dream, to fight the unbeatable foe, to bear with unbearable sorrow, to run where the brave dare not go … to be willing to march into hell for a heavenly cause, and the world will be better for this, that one man strove with his last ounce of courage to reach the unreachable star.

So he sings his song with Sancho at his side, and the people make fun of him. They say, "What a nut! He's crazy."

Finally, the Man of La Mancha says, "Who's crazy? Am I crazy because I see the world as it could become, or are you crazy because you only see the world as it is? I have come to the conclusion that the dreamer is not crazy, because it is only the dreamer who ever becomes the lifting force in this world."

Now the scene changes, and here they are at the Wayside Inn. The camel drivers are drinking whiskey until dawn. The harlot Aldonza, enters and flirts with the camel drivers as they flirt with her in return, deals are made. The Man of La Mancha sees her, and he says, "Her hair so disheveled, her breasts are so bare." Then he looks at her and says, "My Lady, you will be my Lady. In fact, I will give you a new name. I will change your name from Aldonza to Dulcinea." With this name change from Aldonza to Dulcinea, the Man of La Mancha was using the power of posthypnotic suggestion, which means: I am not what I think I am, I am not what you think I am, but I am what I think you think I am.

The Man of La Mancha is setting in motion, the Psychological Laws of Dynamics. Remember what Jesus said: "You are the salt of the earth, you are the light of the world." Returning to the dialogical discussion between the Man of La Mancha and Aldonzo, he says to her, "My Lady, remember you are My Lady."

Then she looks at him. She spits, laughs, and says, "Don't call me your lady. I was born in a ditch by a mother who left me there cold, ragged, and hungry, hoping that I would have the good sense enough to die. So don't call me your lady. I am only Aldonza, nothing at all."

Then she runs off the stage, and as he reaches out to her, he repeats, "Remember you are My Lady."

Now the final scene that bought me to tears as the curtain opens: The stage is empty and bare, and suddenly, rushing onto the stage is this beautiful Spanish queen wearing a lace mantilla over her dress. The Man of La Mancha is dying of a broken heart, and to his bedside comes this Spanish queen. As she kneels, she offers a prayer, saying, "My Lord."

And he says, "Who are you?"

She answers, "My Lord, don't you remember me? You sang a song, "The Impossible Dream" ...

> to dream the impossible dream, to fight the unbeatable foe, to bear with unbearable sorrow, to run where the brave dare not go ... to be willing to march into hell for a heavenly cause, and the world will be better for this that one man strove with his last ounce of courage to reach the unreachable star.

"You gave me my new name. You changed my name from Aldonza to Dulcinea."

Oh, my friends, she was born again. Her name was changed. Is not this the thing that our Lord wants us to do? See a problem and solve it; find a hurt and heal it? I am reminded of the words of the late Sen. Ted Kennedy who said as he eulogized his brother, the late Robert Francis Kennedy who was gunned down by an assassin's bullet, "My brother need not be idolized anymore in death than he was in life. But he should simply be remembered as a good, kind, and decent man. A man who saw wrong and tried to right it. A man who saw sickness and tried to heal it. A man who saw war and tried to stop it. Some men see things as they are and ask, 'Why?' I dream dreams that never were and ask, 'Why not?'"

— Relentlessly Pursuing Perfection —

Bart Starr is a Hall of Fame quarterback who played for the Green Bay Packers. He played intercollegiate football under the tutelage of the great Paul Bear Bryant at the University of Alabama. The Crimson Tide football team has won a number of NCAA championships over the years. I remember watching Coach Bryant as he paced the sidelines, wearing his herringbone hat tipped to one side. Bart Starr was drafted as a quarterback by the Green Bay Packers. During his first year with the Packers, they only won one game and lost twelve.

The owner of the team became very distressed, dismayed, and disturbed over the Packers' losing record—so much so that he called together all of his executives, scouts, players, and coaches. And He told them, "Men, we can't keep losing like this. We can't keep going on like this. Something has got to be done to change our losing situation."

So they organized a search committee and went out across the highways, byways, hills, valleys, towns, cities, and counties in search of a coach who could help put a winning strategy in place. They found a candidate who met the coaching criteria that they thought could put their team on the winning track, so they interviewed and hired him. The first day on the job, this first-year coach called together all of the executives, scouts, players, and coaches and said, "Gentlemen, beginning today, we are going to relentless pursue perfection." Then he added, "Players, if you are not willing to pursue perfection, go home. Coaches, if you are not willing to pursue perfection, go home." Then he hesitated and said, "Now we all know that we are not going to ever catch perfection, because nothing is perfect. But we are going to pursue perfection because in pursuing it, we are going to catch excellence."

Now the man who coined these words was none other than the

late, great coach Vince Lombardi. Vince Lombardi was a staunch Roman Catholic who relied on his faith and prayers to fulfill his personal and professional needs. I suspect that some of us would look at Roman Catholicism as a cult. Now I don't know about that. All I know is Vince Lombardi went to mass every day and was a man of faith. He was not like some Christians I know who only go to church on Thanksgiving or Christmas or Easter Sunday wearing all of those new clothes and bringing undisciplined children who run around the church, tearing up the hymn books and making a lot of unnecessary noise.

I'm getting ready to make up something here. No one told me this. I have never heard this before, and I have never read this scenario in any book. I am making this up or, as our black forefathers would have said, using my holy imagination, and I must remind you, as a Christian, that my holy imagination always works for me.

Remember that Vince Lombardi was down at the Catholic Church praying, and he thought that he was all alone. But he was not all alone, because the Holy Spirit was down there with him. I know the Holy Spirit was there with him, because the Bible says if you lift your eyes to the hills, help will come.

Not only was the Holy Spirit down there with Vince, but the Apostle Paul was also down there with him. Now remember, I am making this up. The Holy Spirit called Paul, and Paul answered, "Yes, Lord."

The Holy Spirit replied, "Paul, would you say a word to Vince for me?"

Paul answered, "Yes, Lord. I will be happy to."

Now remember that Vince thought he was all alone. Then Paul called Vince and said, "Vince."

And Vince answered in a shocked, startled, and astounded voice as he responded, "Oh ... What? Who ... Who is that calling my name? I thought I was all alone down here."

And Paul said to Vince, "If you want to get your Packers on a winning streak, tell them they must press toward the mark."

Paul said to Vince, "The Holy Spirit told me to tell you that if you want to get your Packers on the winning track, tell them they must press toward the mark. Tell them as they press, some days are going to be dark, stormy, cloudy, and hazy, but just keep on pressing. Tell them that some days as they press, the lightning is going to play a zigzag game across God's vast horizon, but they must keep on pressing. Tell them as they press some days the thunder is going to roar as a million resounding drums, but keep on pressing, because after a while, if they keep on pressing, they are going to have a breakthrough. And when you have a breakthrough, you are going to hear the owner of the team say, 'Well done.'"

The owner of the team is synonymous with the owner of the universe ... as found in the Holy Bible. His master said to him, "Well done, good and faithful servant; You have been faithful with a few things; I will put you in charge of many things. Come and share your master's happiness!" (Matt. 25:23 NIV).

Now listen to me very carefully, more than forty years ago, Vince Lombardi and his Packers won their division and the playoffs, and they stomped the Kansas City Chiefs into the ground and won the world's first Super Bowl in 1967. During the next year, they defeated the Oakland Raiders and won the world's second Super Bowl in 1968.

At the beginning of every preseason training in the National Football League, the goal of every team in the league (all thirty-two teams) is to win the Vince Lombardi Super Bowl Trophy. The most prestigious trophy in the NFL is not a conference trophy; it is not a divisional trophy; it is not a pro bowl trophy; it is not the most valuable player trophy. The most prestigious trophy is the Vince Lombardi Super Bowl Trophy.

Vince Lombardi's name became synonymous with success in the National Football League all because of one man who took a losing team and said to the owner of the team, the players, the executives, and the coaches, "Gentlemen, beginning today, we are going to *relentlessly pursue perfection.*" That man was none other than the legendary Vince Lombardi. The Vince Lombardi Super Bowl Trophy is as recognizable in the NFL as the name John Fitzgerald Kennedy, the thirty-fifth president of the United States, is recognizable to Americans.

—— My Chronological Appointments ——

My chronological appointments where I spiritually served for nearly forty years are listed below.

1965–1966: Mt. Zion Methodist Church, Clearwater, Florida

1966–1967: Stewart Memorial Methodist Church, Daytona Beach, Florida

1967–1968: Wilson Temple Methodist Church, Raleigh, North Carolina

1968–1975: John Wesley United Methodist Church, Fayetteville, North Carolina

1975–1995: Commissioned, US Army Chaplin (two years active duty and eighteen years Army Reserve)

1977–1986: Wesley United Methodist Church, Los Angeles, California

1986–1988: Scott United Methodist Church, Pasadena, California

1988–1991: Holly Park United Methodist Church, Gardena, California

1991–2001 (retired): Grace United Methodist Church, Los Angeles, California

Four Heartwarming Experiences

Experience 1

My First Ministerial Appointment

here were four experiences that happened to me personally during my more than forty years of active ministry. I shall begin by sharing the first of my heartwarming experiences that began during my 1967 appointment as pastor of a small all-black church named Wilson Temple Methodist Church, which was located in Raleigh, North Carolina. Rev. Vernon Tyson invited me to be his eleven o'clock service preacher at his all-white congregation. I was being transferred from the all-black Florida Conference of the Central Jurisdiction to an all-black North Carolina Conference just prior to the merger with the Evangelical Brethren United Church and the Methodist Church that became the United Methodist Church.

We all know that the 1960s were a dangerous time for blacks and whites to be mingling and mixing together. Dr. Timothy B. Tyson, Ph.D, son of Rev. Vernon Tyson captures the event of his father's invitation for me to be his eleven o'clock worship service preacher at his all-white congregation in Oxford, North Carolina. This happened in 1967, not too long after the 1964 murders in Philadelphia, Mississippi, of James Chaney, Andrew Goodman, and Michael Schwerner who were three civil rights workers and the 1963 assassination of civil rights activist Medgar Evers in Jackson, Mississippi. There was a bombing, killing Addie Mae Collins, Cynthia Wesley, Carole Robertson, and Denice McNair, four little girls in Birmingham, Alabama, at the Sixteenth Street Baptist Church. There was also another situation involving Viola Gregg Liuzzo who was murdered during a voter registration incident that occurred in 1965 in Selma, Alabama. You must know that these were not the only deaths during 1963, 1964, or 1965, but they were all recorded as significant deaths during these trying times.

Now, I mention these deadly situations because they all happened just a few years before my 1967 invitation to preach in Oxford, North Carolina. Yet Rev. Vernon Tyson was willing to put his life on the line even though there was a strong possibility of him losing his appointment as pastor of Oxford Methodist Church, his livelihood, and even his life because he chose to invite a black man to preach in his all-white congregation.

Rev. Vernon Tyson's son, Dr. Timothy B. Tyson, professor of Afro American Studies at the University of Wisconsin–Madison, captures so magnificently in his awesome book *Blood Done Sign My Name* on pages 103, 104 105 records the events surrounding his father's invitation to Rev. Gil Gillespie to come and preach at the eleven o'clock worship service at his all-white congregation.

Dr. Timothy B. Tyson started out by writing the following:

> His Daddy went back to the well in 1967 and once again invited a black preacher into his pulpit, thinking that things had probably eased up a little since the Dr. Proctor episode in Sanford, North Carolina. He had survived that one and after the waves of race riots in the intervening years, Daddy probably figured that a black man in the pulpit would not seem so revolutionary. In this case, when Daddy told Eli Regan, his powerful lay leader, that he was planning to invite Reverend Gil Gillespie, a noted black Methodist preacher, to deliver a sermon at our church, Regan asked why Daddy wanted to do a thing like that. "Racism was an important moral issue," Daddy replied, "an issue that the church needed to confront." He went on to say "putting a black man in a position of honor and authority in front of a white congregation was a good thing, and if there was a controversy over it, that was not a bad thing, either. People needed to work through these things, and not just in the abstract."

The wizened old conservative responded that he didn't think racism was a problem in our church at all; that he'd never heard that racism was a problem in our church and, that he'd never heard anything that suggested any antipathy toward "our <u>nigrah</u> brothers and sisters." Had Vernon asked anyone on the administrative board whether they thought this was a good idea? No, Daddy told him, the Methodist *Book of Discipline* stated clearly that the minister shall determine the number and nature of services. And he didn't need to take a poll to know how people felt about these things. Nor did he think that a minister was bound by the principle of majority rules in all cases. Did the preacher mind, Regan wanted to know, if he asked around a little bit? Daddy told his lay leader that he didn't mind him asking around, as long as Regan understood that as a preacher he had to do what the Lord called him to do.

Regan dropped by the office the following day. "Vernon, you've only been here a year and you know us better than we know ourselves," he said. "I asked almost everyone on the administrative board, and you don't have one bit of support for bringing in that <u>nigrah</u> preacher. I don't think you have one vote, if it came to that," Regan said. For a moment, it seemed as though the conservative elder was preparing to warn Daddy not to invite Reverend Gillespie to speak. "We need him a lot worse than I thought we did," Regan went on. "You bring him on, and don't you back down on it, either. I'm not going to say a damn word about it unless you get in trouble," he said, "I might even oppose you a little bit. But if they come after you, they will have to come through me first." And then the red-faced old man winked at him, and ambled out the door and went back down to the orphanage.

When the news of Reverend Gillespie's coming filtered out to the congregation, there was a fair amount of low grumbling, but nothing approaching the protests in Sanford before Dr. Proctor came. And while Reverend Gillespie never became a nationally known orator and intellectual like Dr. Proctor, he was steeped in a black Southern homiletic tradition and was one hell of a preacher. Reverend Gillespie had all the traditional strengths and the polish of a good education too and a smile that would melt glass. His personality was so forceful, as folks back home say that if he'd drowned in the river, folks would have looked for the body upstream. He was the genuine article, a first-class, grade A "pulpit peacock," as my father and his five preacher brothers would put it.

WOXF (the local radio station) routinely broadcast my father's sermons locally, so that shut-ins, the elderly, and those members whose Sunday morning could not transcend their Saturday nights could hear the Word nonetheless. That morning, Daddy hadn't notified WOXF that he would not be preaching. And so when Reverend Gillespie climbed into the pulpit, he was unfurling his words not merely for the white congregation in front of him, but for all of Grandville County. Otto von Bismarck had a point when he warned the Reichstag that conquering armies were not halted by the power of eloquence, but he had never heard Gil Gillespie. That morning my father's controversial guest was like the minister who, as the poet Richard Baxter once wrote, "Preached as never to preach again, and as a dying man to dying men." Gillespie simply mesmerized everyone in the congregation and, for all we knew, everyone in the county who had a radio.

Daddy's most implacable adversary on the question of inviting Reverend Gillespie had come to Sunday school earlier that morning. But the fellow made a point of letting my father know that, as "a matter of principle," he was not staying for the eleven o'clock worship service. The next week however, the man dropped by the church office with a confession. "Vernon," he laughed, "I started on home, but I reckon I have more curiosity than I do principles because I could not keep myself from turning on the radio in my car just to see what the man was going to say." As he drove along, the fellow told Daddy, that he became more and more intrigued by the sermon and almost forgot who was giving it.

"When I got to the house," he said "I couldn't get out of the car because he was still going at it. My wife just brought me out a sandwich and laughed at me." The man threw back his head and squealed at his own silliness. "I'll tell you, Vernon," he said, "the longer that feller preached, the whiter he got." Even though Reverend Gillespie's 1967 visit caused less trouble for my father than Dr. Proctor's had in 1964, it would be a mistake to assume that the racial chasm in American life had narrowed. In fact, few white people, North or South, were comfortable with the notion of racial equality in the early 1960s.

Experience 2

A Dream Come True

The most gratifying event was an actual dream come true for me when God almighty confirmed my appointment from 1977 through 1986 at Wesley United Methodist Church in Los Angeles where He later provided me "The Love of My Life in Holy Matrimony ... Barbara Bonney." These dedicated words, written in this book *The Lighthouse of Words*, would not have materialized without the inspiration of my Barbara. You will find my words of affection for her in my dedication to her on page 7 in the My Family section of this book.

My Spiritual and Military Service Roles

*M*y appointments continued even while I served in the US Army as an army chaplain. I was likewise in a very different but most rewarding duty of service. There were many troops within the military who had immediate needs that required kindness, compassion, and a personal element to enhance their ability to serve.

Prior to the 1975 session of the North Carolina Annual Conference, I asked the late Bishop Robert Blackburn if he would permit me to explore the possibility of entering the US Army as chaplain. Reluctantly, Bishop Blackburn granted me my request. After being examined thoroughly by the Commission of Chaplains in the United Methodist Church, which was headed up by the late Dr. Parnell Bailey and Dr. John Wesley Jack Hayward, I was accepted by the US Army Chaplaincy. This acceptance required that I enroll in a nine-week Chaplain's Basic Course at Fort Wadsworth located in New York City.

Following my basic course, I was assigned to my permanent duty station at Fort Ord located in Monterey, California. Fort Ord was called the country club of the US Army because of its great location on the beach of the Pacific Ocean and the fabulous views of Pebble Beach, Carmel, Presidio of Monterey, Seaside, and Pacific Grove.

I was well received at Fort Ord, being the only African American in the midst of some twenty or twenty-five other chaplains. In fact, after about six or seven months as chaplain of Patton Park Chapel, the post chaplain (who is the boss of all chaplains on post), Chaplain Colonel Shaw, called me to his office to encourage me that if I continued to preach and minister to my troops as he thought I was doing, I perhaps someday would become chief of chaplains (major general) in the US Army. However, in the following two years of active duty, I was one of the persons contacted by Bishop Charles F. Golden to fill the vacant pulpit left by Rev. Dr. Robert Smith who was being appointed as superintendent of the San Diego District of the United Methodist Church. I remember the late Bishop W. T. Handy saying to me, "Boy, if the bishop offers you Wesley UMC, take the church and tell your family about it later."

When I talked with the post chaplain at Fort Ord, Chaplain Shaw was very disappointed and saddened by my request to become the senior pastor of Wesley United Methodist Church (the mother church of African American United Methodism) on the West Coast, which is located in Los Angeles, California. He did, however, agree to release me but suggested that I go immediately into the US Army Reserves, and I agreed to follow his suggestion.

I became a monthly weekend warrior serving the troops. I counseled young men and women, many of them who were simply trying to find themselves. I performed marriages, presided over graveside services, taught Bible studies, and walked through storm after storm with my troops and commanders for eighteen years before retiring from the reserves as Chaplain Major Gillespie in 1995.

My Final Appointment before Retirement

Grace United Methodist Church

*M*y final active ministry, where I served ten years as senior pastor at Grace United Methodist Church in Los Angeles was simply a heavenly experience for both me and my late wife, my Barbara, who only spent three of those ten years with me before the Lord called her home in 1994. The following reflections are the expressions from some colleagues, as well as some devoted members and friends whose stated snapshots signify my impact on them during my ministry while at Grace United Methodist Church.

Did you ever see life experiences flowing from a Lighthouse? Just imagine currents of alienation running to find a place within a young child's heart where they could find refuge in scriptures that circle the elements beginning with their childhood. That is where my strength comes from and what has led me throughout my life and beyond. You will see this same image reflected by some actual church members during my spiritual journey from abandonment to divine anointment, some eight decades later.

The Church Motto
Where Jesus Christ is the Star and the Bible takes Center Stage.

The Theme Scripture
Philippians 4:6–7: "Be careful for nothing; but in everything by prayer and supplication with thanksgiving, let your requests be known unto God. And the peace of God, which passeth all

understanding, shall keep your hearts and minds through Christ Jesus."

My retirement begins on the following pages with some personal statements from persons who were members within some of my previous pastoral congregations.

My Retirement Tribute to Grace United Methodist Church and some Personal Reflections from Members and Friends

A Grandmother's Thoughts
Joyce A. Lamkin, Member
Grace United Methodist Church

*R*ev. Sylvester T. Gillespie was always focused on spiritual inspiration during his service of ten years as our pastor at Grace United Methodist Church in Los Angeles. As members, we always remember his teachings that remain an essential part of his ministerial legacy. The weekly sermons were always filled with the Holy Spirit, and we found ourselves retaining the Word of God along with the teachings of the Holy Bible study sessions that were filled with unlimited wisdom.

The theme scripture may be found in Philippians 4:6–7, and it continues to be used during each worship service (even after his retirement) and is memorized, testified, and recited as a spiritual source of motivation in our daily lives. This practice serves as an enhancing guideline in the personal lives of those who strive to live according to the teaching of his pastoral leadership, human kindness, and concern that is displayed throughout his ministry. As a result of his leadership, there was always membership growth of seniors, couples, young children, young adults, and babies throughout his tenure. You, Reverend Gillespie, my brother in Christ, will long be remembered as the pastor who always was eager to lead his flock with God's holy blessings for which we give thanks. I personally appreciate your allowing me to assist you with this project!

A Grandson's Memorable Views
Vernon L. Sance III, Member
Grace United Methodist Church

Reverend Gillespie has always done an excellent job of delivering the gospel, and as a youngster when I heard the word from his sermons, I would leave the sanctuary feeling motivated and armed to conquer my school week ahead. I always thoroughly enjoyed receiving the word from Pastor G because his energy was absolutely contagious. His ability to make his message easy to understand (even for youngsters) and the manner that he makes certain scriptures related to the current events and situations that we experienced in our daily lives are qualities that many others (ministers and pastors) in his same position lack.

I don't actually remember memorizing the theme scripture, but I do remember saying it each day. When I began driving at fifteen years of age, my grandmother insisted that each day before starting my car and driving off that I would say the theme scripture and the prayer of serenity. I shall remain eternally grateful to God almighty for my early spiritual learning resulting from Pastor Gillespie's teachings.

My Theme Scripture Inspiration
Betty Anderson, Member
Grace United Methodist Church

I will always remember Reverend Gillespie as an outstanding teacher of God's word. I credit him with a large percentage of my spiritual growth. When he was pastor of Grace United Methodist Church, his sermons came straight from the Bible. He encouraged every member to bring their own Bibles from home to church every Sunday and be prepared to participate in the Sunday service if he called on you.

Reverend Gillespie insisted on us taking notes and using our Bibles to study the word of God. To this day, I still have my many books of notes from most of his sermons. When I reread some of them, it is like listening to him in person. He believed in following the scripture, and that made it easier for me to read with more understanding. Thanks to Reverend Gillespie, there were many Sundays when I could hardly wait to get home and go over my notes and read the Bible with a clearer understanding. Some Sundays his messages were so powerful and Spirit-filled I would find myself crying and praising God in the car on my way home from church. He was not only a good teacher, but he also encouraged us to step out on faith.

Reverend Gillespie is the reason I got involved in some of our church ministries. I was very shy, but he instilled in me a you-can-do-it attitude. It is with thanks to Reverend Gillespie for his encouragement and confidence in me so that I am now able to stand before the congregation as one of the church liturgists. The most important thing he gave us when he was our pastor was the theme scripture, Philippians 4:6–7. He insisted every member should learn it and be prepared to recite it if called upon to do so. After all these years, the theme scripture is still a part of our Sunday services and a part of my life. When I am stressed or overly concerned about something, I recite the theme scripture, and it gives me inner peace. Thank you, Reverend Gillespie, for sharing your wisdom with us. What a legacy! Love and blessings to you forever!

A Look at Pastor Gillespie's Life
Randolph Washington, Member
Grace United Methodist Church

It is with justifiable pride that I share a major portion of my spiritual journey involving the teachings and directions of Rev. Sylvester T. Gillespie. One might ask, "Who is this man?" I can and will say that he is a man of God. For directions, I reached into my treasure of sermons and Bible study articles that goes back as early as 1991. There are several books of notes from Wednesday night Bible study with forty to fifty people attending on a regular basis. Also, I have retained numerous church bulletins. I must share some notes from a Bible study class dated February 15, 1995, titled "The Authority of a Believer." We were encouraged to understand our role as God's role. God asked us to exercise our authority, and He will do the healing. God is helping us to be obedient and trust in Him.

One sermon titled "The Erosion of Life" continues to be a focal point in my spiritual journey. The primary focus was on handling the thoughts that enter our mind. The process of thought was (1) enter, (2) examine, (3) entertain, (4) enjoy, and (5) experience. What did this message do for me? Subsequently, due to his being away, I was honored to speak at a Sunday service. I chose to revisit this message.

Having been spiritually grounded, I realized through fervent prayer that I could at least examine our thoughts. The Holy Spirit having been revealed, that we can examine and decide whether or not to enter certain thoughts. To have this treasure of sermons and Bible study notes is a blessing. The memories go on and on and on.

We were blessed and honored to have him share our space with the entire congregation. It was a privilege to be a part of Sunday services. Questions and answers after the sermon, the involvement of the youth, and the importance of having your personal Bibles as a weapon. A specialty was to be a part of his sharing with the Methodist men as a friend, mentor, and the true messenger of God almighty. It is a challenge trying to put all of my thoughts into this brief summary. But it is without an effort to answer this question: Why is this man? The answer is this: Pastor Sylvester T. Gillespie.

I am exceedingly blessed to call Reverend Gillespie, My Dear Friend
Gail Blake-Smith, Former Member
Grace United Methodist Church

I am pleased to share my personal insights and experience resulting from my spiritual relationship with Pastor Gillespie. Why? Because he is our former pastor/leader, and he had an army of great friends who loved and honored him. Moreover, many of these past friendships have been maintained with him over the years. I have been blessed to know him for more than twenty years. Not only was he my anointed pastor who taught us how to apply biblical truths to our lives in a way that really made sense, but also over the years, he has become a very special friend.

When I need prayer or encouragement, he is my go-to person! I can also say that Pastor Gillespie deeply loves the Lord and the people whom he has brought into his life. He is also a very gifted communicator and writer. He has a way to take simple concepts and add creativity and poetry to them. I am exceedingly blessed to call him my dear friend!

My Spiritual Father
John Woolery, Former Member
Grace United Methodist Church

To my pastor, Rev. Sylvester T. Gillespie, I love you. You are my father in God's ministry: my spiritual daddy. You taught me to "Not be anxious about anything, but in everything by prayer and petition with thanksgiving let my request be made known unto God and may the peace of God which transcends all understanding guard our hearts and minds in Christ Jesus." You trusted me with your flock, which allowed me to grow in my relationship with our Lord. I watched you love your beloved Barbara. In 1998 the doctors gave you two years to live. I watched you mount up on the shoulders of the Lord and confront cancers. I watched you run and not tire, walk and not faint while being brave and courageously steadfast in your trust in the Lord. You waited patiently on your message from our Lord. You understand and show your children the wisdom from God that is pure, peace-loving, considerate, and full of mercy and grace. Pastor, you mean life to me; from you, it was always the Lord that was first in your walk, where "Jesus Christ is the star, and the Bible takes center stage" in your life. To my spiritual father, may the Lord make His face to shine upon you, may the Lord turn His face toward you and give you peace, and may the peace in God be with you always. Love you, Pastor!

Your boy and his wife
Daryl and Tarita Walker, Former Members
Grace United Methodist Church

Dad, it is impossible to fit into just a couple of paragraphs everything that you, Rev. Sylvester T. Gillespie, have meant to us throughout the years. There just are not enough words for me to adequately describe this. But among those words that top the list are pastor, teacher, mentor, coach, counselor, admonisher, consoler, confidant, adviser, intercessor, amazing leader, encourager, awesome friend, and incredible dad!

The pearls and golden nuggets you've deposited into our spiritual banks continually shape our thoughts and transform our lives. You've kept us centered in the word of God and focused on who we are and *whose* we are, to be anxious for nothing, that we're more than conquerors, that we can do all things through Christ, that we are what we do when no one is looking, and so much more. We thank God for giving us the privilege and blessing to have you in our lives. We can't sufficiently describe it, but we have been and will forever be the better for it. You're *priceless*! As a result of Reverend Gillespie's leadership, there was always a steady membership growth, including seniors, couples with young children, young adults, and babies throughout his tenure. You, Reverend Gillespie, my Father in Christ, will long be remembered with much love, reverence, and adoration.

Your Spiritual Daughter
Dandrea Lynnette Safford, Member
Grace United Methodist Church

It is with honor that I write about my pastor, Rev. Sylvester T. Gillespie! As I reflect upon the impact he has had on my life, I can speak a million and one words about all he's done for me. I met Pastor at the young age of twelve. His dedication and authenticity to the Word of God inspired me in a number of ways.

It is because of him that I gave my life to Jesus Christ. His presentation of God's Word was so real and true. He influenced me, a young teenage girl, to spread the Word of God to my peers. Yes, I was ridiculed and turned away by many of my peers; however, there were a few who were open to hearing the Word of God. As a result, they began to come to church to witness the power and the anointing upon my pastor. I remember how he'd tell me and all the other teenagers, "I want all of my babies sitting right up here on this front pew and taking notes also." And we would all be there, attentive students learning about the power of God. Now, when you can get teenagers to love the Word of God, you've got a true spiritual anointing, and Pastor Gillespie was our spiritual father. We loved him as our father.

I am now thirty-six years old and a mother of a teenage daughter and a preteen son, and I tell them stories about Pastor and how he impacted my life, and they both are in awe of the way he has been such an influence on my life … even still today. Thank you, Pastor Gillespie, for loving me through my good and my not-so-good times. Thanks for your spiritual guidance, because in my hardest times, I was able to remember how you always said, "Lean on God's Word," and that got me through times when I thought I wasn't going to make it. I love you, Pastor! You are a true warrior of Jesus Christ!

Our Profound Leader
Virgil and Helen Jones, Members
Grace United Methodist Church

It was a pleasure having Pastor Gillespie as our wonderful leader. In each of his sermons, he reminded us that God is still on His throne, and all we have to do is call upon Him in times of trouble. He was a constant reminder to us to be thankful for what God has done for us. His weekly sermons gave us hope to guide us through the following week. He constantly reminded us to be obedient in the Word, and to look unto our heavenly Father to supply all our needs according to his riches in glory. We have a deep appreciation for what pastor Gillespie has done in our spiritual lives.

There was a group of younger boys attending the church while Reverend Gillespie was our pastor, and at first, they sat in the back of the church. The pastor wanted them near him; he would insist that they move nearer the front, and he would spend time teaching them, helping them and guiding them, especially the fatherless youngsters. He called them his babies, and if one of them would fail to come to church, he would call them, talk to them, and insist that they return to church on the next Sunday because he needed to see their smiling faces. His technique worked because they simply obeyed him.

Another group of his congregation that was special to him was the senior citizen members, and he was instrumental in having a handicapped lift installed for the convenience of the older members. He was such an inspiration to all of his members, and the Lord blessed him during his administration at Grace United Methodist Church. My wife and I are grateful and want to thank Pastor Gillespie for his devoted service to all of the members. He has blessed us all to see a brighter sun. May God's blessings continue to be with you, Reverend Gillespie ... this day and always.

Memorable Moments of Our Pastor
John and Thelma Mayes, Members
Wesley United Methodist Church

Pastor Gillespie came into my life in the 1970s. At that time, he officiated the funeral of my mother who was a member of Wesley United Methodist Church. During those years he ministered to the members of Wesley Church is when our relationship began. I was a young man trying to develop spiritually and was helped and mentored by several members of the church. As the years went on, even though he was assigned other appointments, our relationship continued. I was especially impressed with his preaching and teaching. After you left, you still retained something from the message that you could apply to your life.

As I look back over the years, I saw him progress even though his marriage ended. He continued to move on, serving the Lord, preaching the Word, and leading his flock. But as time passed on, I saw a new spark of life within him after he later met and married Barbara ... the special love of his life. His life jettisoned as if it were a rocket from that point on.

I was still maturing as he mentored me. He allowed me to

conduct Bible studies even though I was not seasoned yet. However, as the years moved on and I became more proficient in the Bible as I attended Bible teaching schools, I was able to research and assist him with scriptures when he needed a particular one. I was always delighted when I followed him to visit other churches where he was appointed as pastor. He never failed to acknowledge my presence, and I was always honored when he referred to me as my professor. To this very day, he continues to keep in touch with me and my lovely wife, Thelma Mayes. To this very day, he will always be *my* pastor.

Inspired by God's Best
Curtis and Yolanda Parrish, Former Members
Grace United Methodist Church

As a married couple, we are fortunate that our parents planted the seed that began the journey of our relationship with Jesus Christ. However, it was during our time at Grace United Methodist Church in Los Angeles, California, which was then pastored by Rev. Sylvester T. Gillespie, that our understanding of the Bible and our yearning desire to learn more gained momentum. Pastor Gillespie was able to break down the barriers of learning and understanding by applying the Christian principals, taken straight from the Bible, to everyday life. That made it real to us, and it provided a platform for an even deeper relationship with Christ, leading to our consistency in seeking the Word of God in all that we do. We are forever grateful for the wisdom and for the life lessons that were taught by our spiritual father on Earth, Pastor Gillespie. My young adult son continues:

Cammeron Parrish

I was christened by Pastor Gillespie when I was an infant at Grace United Methodist Church in Los Angeles, California, where my parents attended worship services. I did not realize it at that time, but as I grew up, Pastor Gillespie would become a major influence in my decision to follow Christ and to be accountable for my actions and words in a way that represents a true man of God. Pastor Gillespie would sometimes speak directly to me as he delivered his sermon, which inspired me to stay in the Word and to always reach for excellence in all that I do.

The Beginning of a Lifetime Journey
Debbie Sanders, Former Member
Grace United Methodist Church

My Dearest Pastor Gillespie: You and I have a very special bond. I am a former member of Grace United Methodist Church. That's where I first heard you preach. I had never heard a pastor bring the Lord's Word with such vim and vigor. It was a delight. You even gave us Greek words to study. As you told us on many Sundays, "Being a Christian is not always easy. There are times when we will have challenges," and that's when you introduced to the Grace Church congregation the theme scripture found in Philippians 4: 6–7. It changed my outlook on life. There are still times when I get a little anxious, but I remember what the Lord told you to tell us. "Be anxious for nothing."

Pastor G., you are a treasured blessing in my life. I am truly grateful for your many teachings and your wonderful friendship. My prayer is that God almighty will continue to give you health, strength, and the great sense of humor that you possess. I am looking forward to hearing many more sermons in the future. May God's blessings continue to be yours forever, and may He always keep you in His loving arms just as you have so graciously instilled in us. I am looking forward to hearing many more sermons in the future. Your daughter in Christ.

Special Sentiments from
Marvin and Pamela Byrd, Members
Grace United Methodist Church

We met Rev. Sylvester T. Gillespie in 1991 when he came to Grace United Methodist Church as our new pastor. He was very instrumental in my growing in my Methodist faith during the ten years he was assigned to Grace. I became active in many areas of our church. In the United Methodist Men's (UMM) Group, I took on the responsibility as president, vice president, treasurer, and secretary. I became a regular participant as a liturgist, even though I hated getting up in front of people and knew nothing about leading a church service. I was on the trustee board, which was a growing experience, as I learned to manage the church property.

On the spiritual side of my time with Reverend Gillespie, I also grew way past my expectations as a church member. I was not much of a Bible study person prior to his coming to Grace, but he told me that he expected to see me on Wednesday nights. Before I knew it, instead of getting in my car and heading home after work, I would find myself heading in the opposite direction—to Bible study. I even found myself often being among the first to arrive and helping to set up the room and getting prepared to take notes. Believe me, before this, I was not a church-going, note-taking person—especially at the Gillespie level of note-taking. The note-taking served me well, because you never knew when in Bible study or church service Pastor would put you on the spot to show your sword (your Bible) or call on you to recite from your church notes. He rarely caught me unprepared. Thank you, Reverend Gillespie, for being part of my spiritual growth at Grace Church.

Our family joined Grace UMC in the mid-eighties; our children were in their early teens when we met Reverend Gillespie and his lovely wife, Barbara, when they were assigned to Grace. The Gillespie's was what our church needed … He was a hands-on preacher, and Mrs. Gillespie was the most gracious first lady with the singing voice of an angel. As previously mentioned, we were very involved in the church. My wife, Pam, served as chairperson of finance and an adult Sunday school teacher. Our children attended Sunday school every Sunday. Reverend Gillespie tried to get as many Grace Church members as possible to become involved in various ministries of the church. He insisted that everyone bring their own Bibles to church, and even though he retired as pastor in 2001, we take notes to this day.

Once our daughter was not at church, and Reverend Gillespie wanted to know where she was. I told him she was home doing her laundry. His reply was, "She has six other days to do laundry. She should be at church today." She has a son of her own now, and they both attend church every Sunday. (Laundry gets done on Mondays.) Our son does not attend church as regularly as he used to, but when it came time for him to get married, he asked Reverend Gillespie to be the officiate, which he did not hesitate to do. Reverend Gillespie has been a very important part of our family's life, and we thank God for him.

From Us to You, Pastor
Kevin Minor, Former Member
Grace United Methodist Church

There is only one preacher of the Gospel of Jesus Christ in the world whom I simply call Pastor. Not Pastor Johnson or Pastor Mike ... just Pastor. The perfect fit that you and your ministry became to my life, as a skeptical new believer, was highly unlikely. I am grateful that at a critical time in my life and career, you became my pastor, my spiritual father, and my friend—a perfect fit to my life.

Your ministry at Grace UMC began with a lot of challenges— the church, the congregation, the politics—and you confronted and addressed them all courageously. You were bold but pleasant, tough but loving, kind but not a pushover, sensitive but not effeminate, effective but not overly demanding, not always right but not afraid to admit being wrong, brilliant but not cocky, loving but not mushy, a servant leader … a perfect ministry fit.

There are but a few ministers of the Gospel who are experts at giving a message in the moment. Preaching, teaching, yielding to the Holy Spirit, and at that same time, that's when spiritual magic happens; people hear from God and get set free from things. It is the type of preaching when more than three hundred people in the Sunday services can feel and believe that your message spoke exclusively to them. I experienced it too many times to call it a coincidence—times when I had been processing an issue all week, only to have you speak directly to that issue, providing the answer along with the scripture to back it up. Your flock was fed, and the word was a perfect fit at Grace.

The attractive culture and vision of your ministry breathed new life into the church—and especially to the youth. You demonstrated Christ's love and inspired them to see who God made them to be, but you did it by keeping it simple; you spoke directly to them and affirmed them. They responded to your lifting them up publicly. The result was a thriving youth ministry, critical to an aging church congregation. Your ministry drew many young in from the outside and presented a brilliant model for growing the church, creating a perfect growth fit.

You, Pastor, through our Lord, managed to overcome significant odds to become the great godly man and leader that you are. My look back at your work shows me that He had you navigate the difficult times of your early life so that He could prepare you to shepherd others through the times of their lives—the good, the bad, and the other—with perfection.

My life is blessed that you chose to go God's way early on. Multitudes have reaped from what God has sown through you, a valiant man of God. I respect you and love you. And my wife goes on to say:

Lolita Minor

Pastor, I can remember my grandmother's (Mary Stevenson) words so vividly, as though it were yesterday. She said to my sister Tarita and me, "When you find a church home and join it, God is going to bless you." Well, she was right! And for those who know us, you know the rest of the story. The decision to join a little church called Grace on a Sunday morning at eleven o'clock in late 1996 brought tremendous blessings into our 1ives.

The most important blessing of all was to delve into the Word of God in a way unlike ever before, under your leadership and awesome teaching. Pastor, your charismatic delivery of the messages you preached, with flair all your own, was life-changing. Your commitment to the Word is unshakable, and the love you give to those you call family is unforgettable. Through the additional blessings of my loving husband, Kevin, who gave me an incredible marriage proposal during a worship service at Grace and two beautiful daughters who love the Lord, Grace has had a huge impact on my life. And having you there to share in it all made it that much sweeter. Pastor, there are people who touch lives, and then there are those who leave their imprint forever on your heart. That's who you are. Thank you for being true to God's Word and for demonstrating the *audacity* of *faith*! We all love you.

Our Pastor's Leadership
Ezunial Burts Jr.
Grace United Methodist Church

In the year 2000, my children, Eze III and Erin, were eighteen and sixteen years old, respectfully. I was working in a high-pressure position as executive director of the World Port Los Angeles, which was the largest and fastest growing port in the United States. At the time, Marion Jean, my bride for more than thirty-one years, was a full time public school administrator. We were both active in church and in the community, serving on various boards and engaging in other local economic development activities. I thrived in my multifaceted role as a church member, a community activist, working professional, and a husband and father. However, when my son graduated from high school and was preparing to venture off to college and into manhood, the advice I would impart and the actions I would take were not as clear as other areas in my life.

Fortunately, my pastor, Rev. Sylvester T. Gillespie, was right there with the answer. One of his messages in particular still rings truth with me. On Sunday, August, 20, 2000, Reverend Gillespie delivered a message titled "Where He Leads Me." The message referenced the scripture of John 6:16–20. This message was particularly significant since it was my son's last Sunday before heading off to USC. There were several broad messages that he laid out:

- Make God your best friend; as you grow up draw closer to God.
- When the waters get rough, keep Jesus in the boat with you.
- Do not worry about life's storms as long as Jesus is your Skipper. Safe ports are ahead of you.

There were three very specific anchors of principals to help you ride out stormy times:

1. Be governed by God's *providence.*
   - God knows your future and what storms are ahead awaiting you; know that He is in control of your storms.
2. *Grow* by God's plan. Learn lessons—benefit—with your life and enlarge your life by God's growth techniques.
   - Work toward *joy,* not just happiness.
   - Thank God that you (or we) were selected to carry certain loads.
3. Be *gladdened* by God's lessons.
   - Appreciate God's everlasting presence with you and know that he will always be your guide.

- Do not be afraid to be happy and joyful.
- And finally, Jesus will come in your darkest hour and give you light.

This message was full of shipping, maritime, and sailing metaphors, which immediately resonated with me. It was easy for me to relate. Most importantly, it equipped me to provide (supply) a young man with knowledge, techniques, and strategies for handling life's challenges and opportunities. Pastor Gillespie continually made my job easier as a man, a husband, a father, and a community leader. And I am forever thankful. Our son's spiritual outlook:

Ezunial (Eze) Burts III

I am honored to contribute to Pastor Gillespie's book, *The Lighthouse of Words*. I believe he embodies the qualities of a Kingdom Man as defined in the book written by Dr. Tony Evans: a kingdom man visibly demonstrates the comprehensive rule of God underneath the Lordship of Jesus Christ in every area of his life. Pastor Gillespie's vision, spiritual counsel, and ability to instill confidence in young people of color are unrivaled.

When I met Pastor Gillespie in 1989, I was an uncomfortably shy youth who experienced difficulty interacting with others in new environments. He was a dynamic, energetic, charismatic, engaging, and inspiring leader serving at the helm of Grace United Methodist Church in Los Angeles. Nearly three decades ago, he immediately struck me as a highly inquisitive community leader, a supreme orator, and a positive role model with innately nurturing instincts. He drew out my strengths, encouraged me to participate in maturity-building activities (serving as a member of the Grace Youth Usher Board), and nudged me into important leadership and public speaking roles (reciting the theme scripture, Philippians 4:6–7, 19 in front of the entire congregation). He also empowered me to develop the self-confidence necessary to feel at ease in unfamiliar territory. My most memorable moment occurred in May 2000 when I graduated from St. Bernard High School and looked back on my journey under Pastor Gillespie's wings. I was fearless about facing my upcoming life challenges, and I felt fully equipped for my next chapter toward my journey to enter the undergraduate student at the University of Southern California (USC).

As a result of being cultivated by Pastor Gillespie, the formerly shy youth has transformed into a global leader who is now responsible for ushering Boeing—a multinational, Fortune 500 company, the world's largest aerospace corporation, and the largest United States exporter— into its second century. In my global engineering leadership capacity at Boeing's corporate headquarters in Chicago, I am responsible for overseeing company-wide strategy and investment levels for global strategic partnerships that promote the Boeing brand, influence external policy objectives, strategically shape industry technical standards, and directly impact Boeing's enterprise engineering and technology strategy. I also impact Boeing's global talent strategy by increasing the retention of impactful aerospace professionals and cultivating an unrivaled diverse talent pipeline to fuel Boeing's second century of innovation. I am involved in various community development organizations that revitalize inner-city neighborhoods throughout the Greater Los Angeles; Chicago; Washington, DC; St. Louis; and Seattle regions.

Serving as a member of the Grace community under Pastor Gillespie's tutelage enabled me to hone my leadership ability while growing up in Los Angeles. My story is not unique by any means. Pastor Gillespie has cultivated many powerful, innovative, educated, and influential global business titans; entrepreneurs; community activists; and game-changing servant leaders. He was widely known for adopting and rescuing young brothers and steering them in the right direction. In the words of Gladys Knight, he was the "wind beneath our wings." Pastor Gillespie has always been passionate about cultivating and deploying the next generation of young, millennial-generation leaders who would go on to be productive members of the Greater Los Angeles region and tackle the most pressing challenges facing our nation. We obtained the blueprint for success from him. Thank you for this opportunity to make this contribution in your book.

A Gillespie Family Groupie
Ruth Conley, Member
Wesley United Methodist Church

My first interaction with Reverend Gillespie was early in his July 1977 appointment at Wesley UMC, Los Angeles. While standing in the narthex of the church, a member mistakenly referred to him as Reverend Smith (his predecessor). He was startled, and he corrected this member immediately, loudly, and sternly by saying, "My name is Sylvester Thaddeus Gillespie." None of us ever made that mistake again.

He continues to be my minister, religious mentor, friend, brother, and confidante, and he has been responsible for my continued development as a church leader. He trusted me to serve as the youth coordinator of his ministry team. Because of his military background and leadership style, he made assignments, allowed you to follow through your task, and expected the leader to report the results to him. He was a delegator, and he did not have a need to micromanage the persons he identified as the leaders of a specific project. Rev. Marvin Andrew Robinson Gaither, who was the youth pastor, and I were able to develop a dynamic youth ministry at Wesley and beyond. Reverend Gillespie's faith in me instilled many useful skills, helping me to serve as youth coordinator in every level of the UMC (local, annual conference, jurisdiction, and nationally Black Methodist for Church Renewal).

I accepted my Gillespie groupie role following his teachings, as well as in observing him at various churches and settings where he continues to be invited for guest preaching engagements. After he served as my pastor, his appointments to other churches, and into his retirement, our relationship is one I cherish. It is my honor to be his accepted as your sister in Christ.

Words of Encouragement from My Spiritual Heroes and others

My Spiritual Counselor
Rev. Dr. Zan Wesley Holmes Jr.

*R*everend Gillespie, after reading your book titled *The Lighthouse of Words*, I am pleased to submit the following endorsement: "I thank God for my co-laborer and friend, Rev. Sylvester T. Gillespie, and his faithful ministry through the United Methodist Church. On this occasion, I am especially grateful that God has inspired him to write his book, *The Lighthouse of Words*, which is a recounting of his life's journey as a disciple of Jesus Christ for the transformation of the church and the world. He is transparent as he shares both his joys and the challenging obstacles that he courageously had to overcome on his journey to reach his God-given potential. He also makes it clear that he has been blessed by the insights, prayers, testimonies, and his stories. I trust and pray that *The Lighthouse of Words* will help brighten the pathways and be a blessing to all who reads it.

—Rev. Dr. Zan Wesley Holmes Jr.
Retired pastor emeritus after twenty-eight years (2002)
St. Luke Community United Methodist Church, Dallas, Texas

My Spiritual Confidant
Rev. Dr. Cecil Leonard Murray

The Lighthouse of Words by Rev. Sylvester T. Gillespie with technical assistance by Joyce Lamkin is destined to launch a renaissance movement in the hearts, souls, and minds of persons in the worldwide search for meaning. The spiritual words resonate within the spiritual souls of all who are engaged in a search for *meaning in what can be a meaningless time.* The spiritual words attach to the spiritual soul with quotes not only from some awesome figures but from some unknown who yet work to make the word become *flesh. The word exceeds mere words, for we do not merely* remember ideas, but recall eternally the ideas made flesh.

In the beginning was the Word, and now the Word has become a lighthouse penetrating the darkness of life. The mother of Sylvester, a child herself, who nonetheless brings a light out of darkness of youth: a light that is delivered from darkness even when the mother disappears for all time. Her son, in a lost and lonely time, endures teasing from peers who are not like the *Good Samaritan* but the bad Samaritans. In spite of all this, he emerges into ministry, a calling inspired by competition with one of his few friends, plus the gift of a Bible from a gracious white businesswoman.

The next stage of growth occurs at age twelve when the first African American bishop elected in the Methodist Church facilitates his enrollment in a Poor Boys' School located in Waveland, Mississippi. The school, designed for poor rural boys, becomes an extended family and guaranteed home and feeding source, in spite of its surrounding by racial segregation—a unique situation for the South.

The walk with God continues. The experience is great. Sylvester literally becomes known as the go-to boy and the cleanup boy. God's dialectic shows: preachers and scholars spent summer months at Gulfside. Then the next miracle: one couple adopts Sylvester as their foster son, loving him as their own, energizing him to go on to Rust College in Holy Springs, Mississippi, from which he graduated in 1962 after serving as president of his freshman and his junior class. Further adding to his bachelor degree, he goes on to Gammon Theological Seminary in Atlanta to achieve his master of divinity degree. He steadfastly prays, giving God the glory for whatever he has become and whatever he will become. From that point come words that can be capsuled in brevity and yet endures for longevity. The distinguished list of words include belief, belonging, church, clever expressions, cutting words, discernment, faith, God, grace, Holy Spirit, important words, inner peace, Jesus, and knowledge.

This story is our story, universal in its application, inspiring in its outcome, strengthening in its process, and looking back as per Reverend Sylvester T. Gillespie, anyone who knows him is walking behind him and hearing the words of wisdom of the heavenly Father, which are: Walk on. Walk on with hope in your heart, and you'll never walk alone. You'll never walk alone. Keep on writing, Sylvester. You have a best seller!

—Rev. Dr. Cecil L. "Chip" Murray
Retired pastor after twenty-seven years (2004)
First African Methodist Episcopal Church, Los Angeles, California

Another Spiritual Leader
Rev. Dr. Robert Habersham

In the creation of heaven and earth, thank God that He created special people like Sylvester T. Gillespie to become one of our ministerial leaders. In Sylvester, He planted a particular seed that bloomed and blossomed and prospered in the proper time and the proper place even though it did not always seem possible for Sylvester to achieve. And this was quite evident through the writing of his book *The Lighthouse of Words* as he describes in detail the data about himself, his joys, his love, his anguish, his disappointments, and even his grief. Only God knows the depth of his journey as he is reminded of his continuing quest toward perfection—to the Glory of God, while he searched for life eternal through it all. And yes, he stills continues to fulfill those purposes that God prepared for him through ... love, devotion, loyalty, and vision. I shall continue to call him *the great one*.

The Ill. Rev. Dr. Sir Robert Habersham 33°
Retired pastor
United Methodist Churches (1958–96)
New York and California
California Pacific Annual Conference
District Superintendent (1980–86)
Director of Ethnic Ministries (1986–89)

My "Best" Spiritual Mentor
Rev. Gary Bernard Williams

Every young pastor needs a spiritual mentor. The question for me was am I willing to reach out and seek the guidance of a mentor? I certainly found one in Rev. Sylvester T. Gillespie. The benefit has been invaluable and has provided me with a lifeline in the sea of storms that spring up in the ministry. Reverend Gillespie has become my father in the ministry. I first became acquainted with his ministry when he was the pastor of Grace United Methodist Church when my wife, Myrna, and I started attending his weekly Bible study. As I walked into the very first class, I was amazed to find more than sixty people in attendance. After joining his class, I soon realized he would become my model on how to do Bible study. He has a wealth of Biblical knowledge with a very engaging personality. Watching him teach the Bible was good practice for me. I have modeled my own classes after what I learned from him.

Reverend Gillespie provided me with an excellent example of a role model that was not only in his talk, but also in his walk. Spiritually, this meant that he led with his life and was commanded by scripture. It is evident that he was led by the Holy Spirit, and he presents a godly role model of Christlike behavior. Seeing a godly life lived out was an invaluable benefit for me as a young person seeking ordination in the United Methodist Church. The *me* generation of today does not widely promote this notion of encouragement to others, but the Bible is clear that we should look out for the needs of others.

I have truly benefited from Reverend Gillespie's proactive encouragement and support because he understands the power and value of critical motivation. I believe today that I am the pastor I have become because of my relationship with Rev. Sylvester T. Gillespie.

Blessings to you, Reverend Gillespie, and know that I shall forever be grateful for all of your guidance.

—Rev. Gary Bernard Williams
Pastor
Saint Mark United Methodist Church, Los Angeles, California

A Spiritual Colleague's Version
Rev. Edward G. Hawthorne

I have known Reverend Gillespie (Pops) for thirty years. He is a pastor and mentor to many pastors, including yours truly. I am humble and honored to offer my brief but self-effacing statement in his book. He has within his spirit and intellectual repository of copious wisdom. He has the wit and intelligence of that famous black poet James Baldwin. He understands the human psyche and meets people where they are irrespective of their station in life. He has the uncanny ability to see a person's heart. He has personally counseled and helped me sort out many difficult situations in my life with wisdom, patience, grace, and compassion. Outstanding book, Pops. Shalom!

—Rev. Dr. Edward G. Hawthorne
Senior Pastor
Calvary United Methodist Church, Los Angeles, California

Contributions along
My Spiritual Journey

*W*ith sincere gratitude, I would like to thank the many persons who participated, in one way or another, by helping me to bring the dream of recounting my life's journey and bringing it to fruition by helping me with the completion of this book. As I contemplated this project for many years, I was blessed to be surrounded by extraordinary people who encouraged me to offer the words of inspiration, encouragement, and moral support at all the right moments.

To Joyce Lamkin for her patience and hard work of taking my words, creative ideas, and sometimes rambling thoughts regarding my life and transforming them into this quality project, which I am proud to share. Without the tireless months, days, nights, and hours that were spent in transcribing my words, inputting the information, and reminding me of neglected critical pieces that needed to be included, I know this memoir would not have been completed.

Special thanks are extended to Missy Spicer for her diligence and assistance in implementing the original CD that began my initial spoken thoughts that were prepared for transcription. To Cynthia Coleman for her ongoing and much-needed editing and revisions from beginning to end. To Betty Anderson for her efforts in finalizing the editing process. To Alice Wilder who provided the clerical computer support in outlining the format that was used in the development of this written manuscript; to Vernon Sance, III for his computer assistance and to Nearly Hernandez for all of her assistance in the printing corrections and the formatting of this manuscript. Also to my fellow clergy, parishioners, and others who cared enough to document their reflections pertaining to my pastoral impact on their lives. Thanks for your kind thoughts confirming that my call to the ministry was not in vain and that it was so ordered by God almighty. I am humbled by your kind reflections and shall always remember your willingness to share your thoughts and assistance in each way that you have seen fit to share with me.

Finally, it is important to remember, as you read each line within this book, my life path from birth until now has created many different courses toward my learning and teachable moments. I shall always be grateful for my going from a perplexing childhood to the tremendous nationwide spiritual family that has shaped me into … the man I am today. Thank You, almighty God, for You so loved me and gave to me a greater life, more than I ever could have imagined or lived to write about.

Benedictions

*M*ay the glow of an Easter Sunrise, the peace of an evening's ending, and the strength of God's eternal hills be your spiritual possession both now and forevermore. Amen.

May God bless you with a cool morning, a warm noonday, a golden sunset, a gentle twilight, and a starlit night, and if the clouds should cross your sky, may God give you the faith to look for a silver lining. Amen.

Do not look back, and do not dream about the future either, because the future will not give you back the past or satisfy your other daydreams. Your duty, your reward, and your destiny are here and now ... Go. You are free. Amen.

Keep your face toward the sun and never look back toward the shadow. Amen.

Our logbook should say this day I will sail on, and every sunset will find me looking forward to a new horizon. Amen.

In Conclusion

*M*y memoir, *The Lighthouse of Words,* is a final ending to a project that has been long in the making. I had been contemplating doing this memoir for quite some time, and it has finally materialized. I believe that the ministry takes many forms and is spread through countless sources of written preparation to reach the masses and is not limited to the pulpit. Many of you may wonder why I undertook this project and what was so important about it. Well, knowing that almighty God had planned my life from birth until now, almost eighty years later, I believe He placed the writing of this memoir on my heart as well. I presuppose there could be many reasons, but what immediately comes to mind is hope, faith, and charity.

It is my hope that when this book is read, many people will spread the word that God's plan for all is hopeful and that a dispirited beginning in life doesn't reflect its final outcome if they turn to God for direction. Personal faith, trust, and patience that God does not make mistakes will reveal many paths forward toward a prosperous and dynamic future. And lastly, even though our lives may many times seem bleak, charity has always been a part of the disenfranchised within our society, and one must hold the belief that charitable persons, organizations, or the wisdom within each of you will open up assistance, opportunity, and a helping hand forward.

While my life certainly wasn't free of sorrow, grief, illness, and day-to-day burdens, I continually reinforced within myself that challenges were a path to growth and that with God, all things are possible. Readers, please know that even in the tough times I was left with my belief that God had an ongoing plan for me. *I may never have been the best at doing anything for the Lord throughout my life, but whatever I have done, I tried to do it well.* Each step of my life's journey has had a precise meaning, lesson, and blessing, and I give eternal gratitude to every life experience as an absolute blessing from God.

I am humbled to have had this opportunity to share my life, thoughts, words, and deeds with each person who has read or who intends to read my memoir—*The Lighthouse of Words*—as well as with those who have shared in some aspect of my life experiences. But to all the rest of my anticipated interested readers who have not yet had an opportunity to read it, I hope that you will. Thank you in advance!

Humbly submitted in this memoir, *The Lighthouse of Words*!

About the Author

$\mathcal{S}$ylvester T. Gillespie is the foster son of the late Bishop Charles and Ida Golden of the United Methodist Church. He graduated from Rust College in Holly Springs, Mississippi, earning his bachelor of arts degree in 1962 and his master of divinity degree was earned from Gammon Theological Seminary of the Interdenominational Theological Center located in Atlanta, Georgia, in 1965. For more than forty years, he ministered, mentored, and lectured in churches and United Methodist colleges and universities across the southeastern United States.

Reverend Gillespie retired from the US Army Reserve chaplaincy in 1995 as a major and from the California Pacific Annual Conference of the United Methodist Church in 2001. He lives in the Baldwin Hills community of Los Angeles, California.

Keynote

All of us need some kind of shelter from the brutal, savage, vicious winds and storms of life. I firmly believe that never before in the history of America have we been so confused, befuddled, and confounded in finding our way out of various dim, dark, and foggy conditions.

The Lighthouse of Words is an attempt to go into the shady, vague, and dark places that have taken up residence in the canyons of our minds because we have allowed ourselves to become overwhelmed and lost in what has become a strange land for us to live in. It is my prayer that *The Lighthouse of Words* will help bring some answers out of our darkness into light and that you will know that I refused to let my life be defined by the horrible experiences of my childhood.

CPSIA information can be obtained
at www.ICGtesting.com
Printed in the USA
BVHW04s1840300418
514863BV00001B/72/P